Become Credit Rich!

From Social Security S.S.I. to Credit Rich

Written by
Bishup Rich Wealth

ISBN: 978-1-959392-36-1

Dedication

I dedicate this book *Become Credit Rich* to my wife, Sarah Mensah, our children, and mother, Rose, and African families, working hard every day to have normal and better lives like everybody else in the world who has to obtain financial freedom for generations to come after me!

I also want to dedicate this book to Miss Scherryl Winston for being my second-greatest cheerleader to see me be successful like a money magnet.

Acknowledgment

I acknowledge Pastor David Crank of the Faith Church in St. Louis, MO. He was an inspiration to me, and one of his messages led me to this path; talking about how credit will make you rich if you know how to use it with discipline!

Contents

About the Author

From a very young age, I always wanted to make a lot of money to do the things I wanted to do without having to work for someone else.

As an author now, I have made this mini book available to the world to let you know there is a way to live a life of abundance and travel the world for yourself while blessing others with your generosity!

The answer is: BECOME CREDIT RICH!

Preface

Having a perfect or high credit score is something that we all dream of, but only a few are able to realize that dream. Building up your credit score can be a herculean task that most people have no clue about. They stumble and fall, trying to navigate and explore the world of credit.

Bishup Rich Wealth is a like-minded individual who wanted to have high buying power, just like his aunt. From an early age, he had seen how his aunt was able to buy him expensive things, all thanks to her high credit power. He, too, wanted this kind of power and so entered the world of credit. Unfortunately, he did not know of the complexities of credits and credit scores which soon landed him with a low credit score. Not being the one to easily give up, he got back on his feet and, through hard work, was able to become credit rich.

Chapter 1: Curious

My auntie Chilly always seemed so rich to me. After all, she could buy anything she wanted whenever she wanted, and she did not have to look at the price tag if she did not want to. I had no idea how she was buying these things and how she bought me a $1200 computer in early 2000 before she passed away in January 2016.

My auntie was amazing to me. I looked up to her because of her financial status and generous giving to friends and family mostly all the time. Auntie Chilly bought me a Roland keyboard six months later that cost $1000 to help me practice my music. I learned how to become my own music producer even though I didn't keep pursuing that dream at that time. But again, I was puzzled because auntie had spent nearly $2200 in that same year on gifts for me alone.

It did not seem like it fazed her at all. So, after seeing auntie prospering like this, I wanted to find out what it took for me to have the same buying power as her.

So now here's my Thuggamony from the T.h.u.g.g. Bishup.

In 2005, I went to a bank in Fort Wayne, Indiana, to start out with a secured credit card with $500. I was only cleared for that amount because my credit was bad. I do not know why I thought I could just walk into that bank and leave that day with a credit card. I really did not know what I was doing at the time, but I just knew that I wanted to be like Auntie Chilly; to buy whatever I wanted, when I wanted to, just like her.

I still did not know about a credit score just yet.

But I felt like the man with that $500 secured credit card. I took my wife shopping to buy new clothes and felt like a real millionaire swiping that card for the first time. I spent the whole $500 on my wife and never paid it off because we divorced soon after, and I moved out of town to Fort Worth, Texas, in 2006. As soon as I made it to Texas, I got with a bank that seemed like they were better than a credit card with their services. They would loan me up to $400 because I deposited my social security check with them each month's direct deposit. That turned out great for me for a whole year until I was ready to move to Dallas, Texas. Then I could not keep up the payments anymore because social security was my only income, and I needed that money to transition to my new apartment, so I left owing them a balance of $440 with interest.

Before I moved to Dallas, I went to court on February 27, 2006, and legally changed my name to Bishop. God was taking me somewhere with this whole thing with credit and my name change, and He would surprise me at the end of December that year. I never could get a credit card with my given birth name, Chris. But suddenly, when I changed my name legally to Bishop, a real credit card came in the mail unsecured for $200, and I had not even applied for it. I was ecstatic that this was happening to me. I spent that whole $200 like it was mine, but this time I would pay my first bill when it came in the mail. The first bill to that credit card was a $20 minimum payment to keep my credit card from being in default. Meaning to say not having a missed payment if you don't know what that means. Or I could pay whatever I want, or just pay off the whole bill of $200. I really thought I was the man for real now. I spent all $200 but only had to pay back a little portion without paying off the whole card.

I met a sister in Dallas who knew about credit, and she told me that I should not spend thirty percent on that card, or it could start messing up my credit. I wasn't trying to hear that because I thought I was doing just fine as long as I made the minimum payment and paid on time.

And just like I thought, after six months or more, the credit card company started asking me if I wanted a credit line increase that would give me more buying power. They would only extend it by another $100, allowing me to have $300, and after the credit line increased that year, I was at $1000 with them. The only thing was, even though I was extended to $1000, I never could enjoy spending that money on the card because I was at my limit with every credit line increase with them already.

A few months later, more credit card offers came in the mail, and I wasted no time applying for them. Unfortunately, they were all small limits of $400. So, I applied for two of them and started spending them up to the limit too, and would pay them on time with the minimum payment and made sure I was not late with them. I did not know what I was doing when I went to a credit union to get a secured loan from them. But when I found out how that worked. It blew my mind when I gave them $500, and then they put that money in a savings account, turned right around, and wrote me a $500 check after I gave them my $500.

But they explained that the next month I would start making $50 payments for the next 12 months until I paid back the whole loan and after I paid everything back to the bank. Then, they would give me back my $500. I wasn't asking any questions because I just left out of that credit union with the same $500 that I was coming to give them in the first place. But I didn't know that I was building my credit profile, which I would find out later. After having $1800 credit that was spent to the limit and just enough to buy little miscellaneous stuff back then, I stepped my game up in California. In 2011, I went to their mall, applied for a Kay jewelers credit card, and got approved for a credit card with them for a $400 credit limit.

I wasted no time once again buying something on it for $100. But at least I did not max out that card because I was not interested in wearing a bunch of jewelry, but I did make sure I was coming back the next month to pay their minimum payment too. That next month when I returned to that mall to pay Kay jewelers their minimum payment, I had to walk through a store called Macy's to get to them. A lady stopped me and asked me.

"Do you want to apply for a Macy's credit card?"

I immediately told her no. I did not think my credit was good enough for this name-brand store that was so hot in New York, where I was from. But she convinced me to apply when she told me that Sean Combs, better known as Puff Daddy, would be in that same mall the next month.

So all I had to do was get approved by them and buy Puff's perfume set called "Unforgettable" for $100 on my credit card. But that was only if I got approved, and I would be one of three hundred people to meet him in the mall in September 2011.

I had nothing to lose looking to meet the most famous Puff Daddy with this big vision and dream I had. So, I told her to run my credit and see what would happen. After one minute, she told me I was approved for $300.

I was so shocked. I hurried up to buy Puff's perfume kit to meet him. The rest of the Puff Daddy story is written in my book called *T.h.u.g.g. Journey part 2 Raw and Uncut* in the chapter called *Rubbing Shoulders with Fame* that you can purchase on Amazon for ten dollars as an e-book and the paperback book for $20.So now I had built my credit file up to $2500 and was still just paying the minimum payments on all five credit cards, making sure I was not late. So all five credit cards gave me $2500 between them, and then I would get another credit card blessing that I did not see coming. I was walking through Walmart when I was approached by another lady asking me to apply for a credit card.

"No problem," I said.

This stuff was getting easy for me after getting all these other credit cards.

I applied confidently, and after a few minutes, I was also approved for a $400 limit with them. Now my credit profile was up to $2900. But as soon as I received the card, I spent most of all my money buying food and paying the minimum payment. The next month when I went to the mall in Cali, I got approved for a JC pennies card for $500. Now I was thinking that my credit report was looking good at this time to get all of these credit cards back to back in such a short time. I wouldn't stop there after having this fun like this. There was a finance company in Tulsa, Oklahoma, that trusted me with $1200 when I visited them in February 2012. So now I started giving away gifts to women on my credit cards in different states that I had never met before but just talked over the chatline telephone to hear their voices. I felt so rich as I was still using up my limits on every credit card that I found out that was called maxing them out! I moved to California in 2011. Because of the cost of living in California, my social security check increased. I got an extra $200 added to my $700 to live on, more than what I would receive in the other states. I had extra money to balance out these credit card payments.

But this would only last for so long. I was only paying the minimum payments on those credit cards. I had an emergency in Fort Wayne, Indiana, with my mother Willa before she died in 2017, and I had to abandon California, which is written in the book chapter called *Burned up. "T.h.u.g.g. Journey part*

2 *Raw and Uncut"* on the Amazon website waiting for you to buy this powerful book for $10 as an E-book, and the paperback is $20! As soon as I left California, my social security check went back down to $700. Now I was in trouble for real because I did not have that extra $200 to keep up with all this bad debt I had attracted by being foolish and dumb with my spending habits with credit cards.

I was not feeling like a millionaire at this time. I felt like a dunce and a failure for being so careless and a bad steward using my credit cards! But I had to do something because I only had two options: pay all those minimum payments or be homeless. After all, I was not on a low income like I was paying for section 8 in California. I was about to throw away all my credit cards to have my whole social security check to live on without stressing about how I would keep up with these credit card payments. It did not take me long to figure out what to do next. I trashed every credit card and kept my sanity and peace.

Chapter 2: Bad Credit

I knew that I was at about a six hundred credit score before I threw away all these cards without paying them again, which made my credit score drop from 100 points to five hundred.

I was living a regular disability life again until God showed me how to start over again, and this time I would discipline my spending habits and learn the true ways of spending on a credit card.

This bad credit card stuff was not going to get the best of me with the new businesses that I had set up in Oklahoma when I moved to this state in 2013.

I was going to win, and I could not see any other way but to fix my credit with all these charge-offs now and derogatory marks that I would reed about on Credit Karma.

Chapter 3: Starting Over

God first showed me how to build positive credit over the negative credit that I had on my credit report. God showed me that if I did that in itself, I would start making my credit look better in due time.

I wasted no time. I went to a bank in Oklahoma City and started with a secured card with a $300 limit this time. But when it got to me, I fought my hardest not to spend over thirty percent and not to max out this credit card. Then I went to another bank which was in a Walmart where I lived and applied for a secured loan like before, and this time I understood that after that whole year, I should have better results with my credit report as I paid over the minimum payments and on time.

Now it's the year 2014, and I kept those payments way above the minimum this time. I even saved $100 each month for the next year to add to my credit card as a credit limit increase. This stuff worked because it took my credit score up to six hundred, and the derogatory accounts on my credit report fell off with help from a credit repair agency that I used for a few months.

I went to Lexington law, where they removed some accounts for me.

By 2015, I was creeping up the ladder again with my credit, even though I now had more than a little bit of negative history.

I took a chance to apply for a capital one business spark credit card and got approved for $1000.

You could not have told me that I wasn't the man on top again. For the next four years, I kept my credit cards in good standing, and after paying my cards on time and early, I stayed at less than what I was told to spend, thirty percent or lower. All of this took me to a credit score of seven hundred by the time I was moved into St. Louis, Missouri, in the year twenty nineteen.

God was about to blow my mind with my new bank. They really loved my credit score and saw that my capital one business card was built up to $3000 at this time.

Chapter 4: High Credit Limit

I spoke to my credit union, applied for one of their credit cards, and got approved for fifteen thousand dollars on the first wop. I was trippin'. I've never had any other bank want to reward me like this, and I knew that I could not mess this up for real.

God was really rewarding me for my discipline and how I have now learned to master these credit cards, put my flesh in check and try not to buy everything just because I could.

The pandemic rose on us by the end of 2019 and early 2020. But I did not let this stop me from being a good steward over this new large limit of credit that was given to me.

I spent so much on this card with Amazon to buy food and stay away from those getting sick and dying because of covid 19. I could pay my balance off quickly that year because I received a $7500 donation to the ministry in 2019, in the summer that I held on to until I got this larger amount of credit.

Six months passed with me having a perfect history with my new credit union, so I asked them for a credit limit increase. I was approved for four thousand dollars to add to the fifteen-thousand-dollar positive credit to make my credit at nineteen thousand dollars of positive credit, and before I could look up, as we say, I had a credit score of seven hundred and forty.

I thought Credit Karma was lying to me. Then I called the real credit bureau trans union to see if this was true, and they told me that I was higher than that at a seven fifty credit score.

Chapter 5: Credit Rich

After seeing myself climb the ladder like this, I applied for another credit card and was approved, this time for twenty-five thousand dollars. I am really becoming credit rich and able to be more of a blessing to other people in lack. This larger limit of credit would come in handy for some of the people I met on Facebook in Ghana, Africa, during this pandemic who were hurting and without jobs to take care of their babies and siblings because of the shutdowns in that country.

The first stimulus check came for twelve hundred dollars when President Donald Trump was still in office. I gave away that whole check to a family in Ghana to have shelter and food.

I felt so good that my credit allowed my non-profit organization, Changed People today INC., to help and give to the less fortunate than us in America.

I applied one last time with my credit union. I was approved for eighteen thousand dollars, which brought my positive credit to sixty-two thousand dollars, with the other credit cards I own with Discover, American Express, and Capital one personal cards with smaller limits. As you read this short story, I have built my credit report to positive seventy-three thousand dollars, and I'm at a perfect eight hundred credit score today.

I had one more thing that I wanted to see myself achieve but this time, not with a personal credit card. I applied in March 2022 to get approved with a business credit card because I needed a real business card that would not report to personal credit. They would only report to business credit profiles and would not lower my score for more significant purchases if I had to make them. They gave me eighteen thousand dollars, which has me at ninety-one thousand dollars positive credit.

The funny part about all this is that I manage all of this credit with a social security check once a month as my stable income that will come once a month for eight hundred dollars.

Thank you, Jesus, for you taught me how to win in the credit game, and become credit rich! LOL

Instructions in This Mini Book Will Get You Blessed, If You Do, What I Did with Excellence with Your Credit Profile Also!

T.h.u.g.g. family and supporters' times are getting really hard in our economy, and you need your credit score right for whets in the near future that we are about to experience.

Paper money is fading away, but your good credit and the word of God will sustain you through these hard times that are getting harder each passing month with mounting prices for food, gas, housing, and so on.

Don't get left out of the credit game when you can get your credit right today!

If this short book registers with you and you want to support this ministry, below is how you donate and give!

Give on our secure website for credit or debit card payments.

www.changedpeopletoday.org

We take Cash app donations at/$Thuggbishup that's a dollar sign/Thuggbishup

Checks or money orders must be written to this address.

Changed People Today.

P.O. BOX 18731

Saint Louis, MO.

63118

Office/314-925-8853

Email/info@changedpeopletoday.org

THUGGALUJAH!!!!!!!

THANKS IN ADVANCE FOR YOUR TIME AND FOCUS ON THIS SHORT STORY!

SINCERELY YOURS,

BISHUP AND SARAH AKUA RICH WEALTH!

Made in the USA
Monee, IL
04 November 2026

67378720R00015

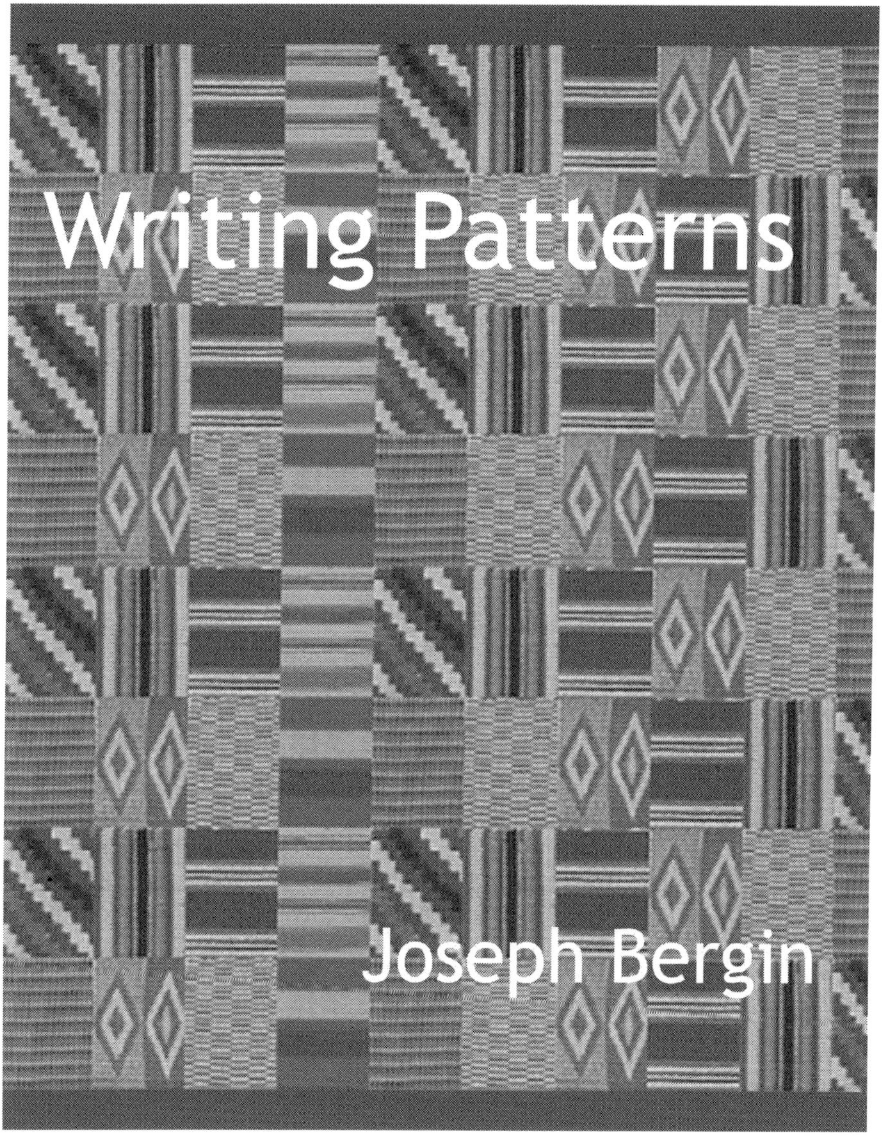
Writing Patterns
Joseph Bergin

Writing Patterns – software, organizational, pedagogical

Joseph Bergin

Published by Slant Flying Press

ISBN 978-1-940113-00-5

The cover image is an amalgam of Kente Cloth patterns. Kente is a West African creation of the Asante and Ewe people. The cover is not a photo of an actual instance, but was created with the online tool at:
http://www.nmafa.si.edu/exhibits/kente/strips.htm.
The colors and patterns of Kente normally convey meaning, though that is not the intent here.

Much of the material here is drawn from the work of the Author. Most of that work can be found at
http://csis.pace.edu/~bergin

Foreword

This book is grew out of a doctoral-level course in patterns. Among the tasks performed by students in the course is developing a set of patterns that work together to solve some problem. We don't require an actual pattern language, but the patterns should build something larger than the results of an individual pattern. This book is derived from the advice I give students on writing and the advice I give them while shepherding their work. It is a personal view, but one gleaned from long involvement in the patterns community.

Another task that my colleague, Fred Grossman, and I require in the course is to apply a set of existing patterns in a real-world situation and report on the results. Students, therefore, get experience both in creating and applying patterns.

The course differs from normal pattern creation in one important way. Most patterns get created because the authors are internally driven to create them. Here the driving force is external. But the results are normally quite good and the papers produced have been welcomed at PLoP for many years. The students also change the way they think about things, such as their research, as a result of the course. Otherwise, the course is similar to the normal "patterns process" in that the student work is shepherded and workshopped within the course. Students are then encouraged to submit their results to one of the PLoP conferences.

As with nearly all work in our doctoral program at Pace University, the tasks are performed in teams. We use patterns, as well as agile principles, throughout the curriculum. One of the agile principles *is just enough*. This is, therefore, a small book. I hope you enjoy it.

Introduction

This is a book about writing patterns: Software Patterns, Organizational Patterns, Pedagogical Patterns, etc. However, it doesn't contain many patterns. It isn't patterns about writing patterns. The material comes from advice I've given students in a course on writing patterns. It hopes to dispel some of the misconceptions about patterns and to ease the creation process. It is not, however, a book about what patterns are. You will need to get that information elsewhere.

The author has written many patterns, including many papers and a few books on Patterns of Agile Practice and Pedagogical Patterns. He is an educator with forty years experience, who is lucky enough to have many colleagues who were present at the introduction of patterns to the software community.

Patterns provide solutions to problems in context.

Patterns provide best practice of experts in a field.

Patterns are only meaningful as part of a Pattern Language.

Patterns are not about research or invention.

Patterns aren't "created." They are "mined" from good practice.

Writing Patterns isn't like Architecture. It is like Archeology.

Writing patterns in your own field can change the way you think about that field. It can make you a better practitioner.

A Pattern has a context, a problem, many forces that need balancing. It has a solution and a resulting context that shows how the forces were balanced and how they were not.

A Pattern Language provides larger and smaller scale patterns to provide context for a given one (larger scale) and help resolve the remaining imbalance (smaller scale).

Writing patterns is an iterative process that includes many people beyond the authors. A well defined "patterns process" brings to bear feedback from many people to enable improvement of the work. A published pattern has likely been revised more than half a dozen times. Some have been revised dozens of times.

Contents

Your Subject

Perhaps you already have a subject to write about. If you do, you will want to first think about whether it is the right subject. If not, you will need to find a subject matter area for your patterns. It will help, in either case, to consider a few characteristics of good patterns.

First, and foremost, patterns are really about creating something. The original patterns were about creating towns and houses (*A Pattern Language*). Organizational Patterns are about creating good organizational structures. Pedagogical Patterns are about creating good teaching structures. Software Patterns are about creating good software structures.

Seen from another angle, patterns are about solving problems that arise in the creation of such structures. Every pattern has a Problem and a Solution. The problem is some inadequacy in the current situation of the world you find (the Context). The solution of the pattern is influenced fundamentally by the Forces at play in that context. The Resulting Context of the pattern describes the changed state of the world, both what has been changed for the better when applying the solution, and what has been left unchanged or left in a worse state. The solution should, at least partially, bring the forces into balance.

A pattern is

a thing (the structure created)

a description of that thing (a piece of literature)

and

a description of how to build that thing (actions taken in the creation).

For example, in the Pedagogical Pattern *Role Play*, the *thing* is a group of students performing a role play. I sometimes use "There was an old lady who swallowed a fly" in a group of students to illustrate list structures in programming. I call it choir practice. Students love/hate it. They think I am so weird, but the lesson sticks.

The *description of the thing* is that part of the pattern that describes what are the characteristics of a role play, and the *description of how to build it* is the solution, telling how to make it work.

So, to analyze your potential subject matter, you can either think about what structures need to be created, or what problems need to be solved in your domain. If you can't think of anything, you don't likely have good subject matter.

Dysfunctional organizations are a good choice. You want to build better organizations.

Poor software practice is a good choice. You want to build a better process.

Poor (or indifferent) teaching is a good choice. You want to improve teaching practice.

Another aspect of patterns is that the expertise needed for best practice in that field must exist and the author must have access to it (or posses it herself). Patterns don't just describe arbitrary solutions, but the best known solutions to their problems.

Format

Format of a Pattern

Patterns can be written in several styles, but there are two main categories: explicit meta-data and implicit meta-data. When starting out you are encouraged to use explicit meta-data as section heads. But at some point, the material might be better represented using various hints rather than explicit names of sections. This is implicit meta-data.

Highly technical patterns are probably best represented with the sections explicitly named. The minimal set of sections is:

Name

Context

Problem

Forces

Solution

Resulting Context

It is also useful to have a *Discussion* section and an *Examples Of Use* section. Others are possible, depending on the subject matter. A picture following the name is very useful. Some treat it as essential. An introductory story to set the stage is helpful, in which case, you should probably continue the story at the end, telling how the issue introduced at the beginning was resolved in the pattern.

Organizational Patterns, and such things as Pedagogical Patterns, being less technical, are probably best represented with implicit meta-data. All of the sections are still there, in the same order, but are introduced with simple typographical and visual cues. For example, the Problem statement can be in italics. The solution can be introduced with "Therefore:" and the rest of the sentence in italics. The context can be separated with a special glyph or icon. You can also limit the context to precisely the first paragraph of what you write. Such a form is more literary and allows easier reading.

In any case, as you begin writing, use explicit meta-data to assure that you don't forget a section. See Traveling Artifact for an example with explicit meta-data and Keep The Ball Rolling for one with implicit meta-data but the same content. Start with the sections mentioned above and add additional sections as you need them. Some patterns work with only a minimal set of sections. Others require more.

I once worked on a pattern language for creating passwords in which the audience was people with some technical sophistication. The problem statements were very short. Even the forces were minimized. It consisted mostly of just solution statements. See Singleton Password for an example.

Format of a Pattern Language

A pattern language is (at least) a collection of patterns that work together and admit "sequences" of patterns that solve problems larger than those of the individual patterns. The presentation of the language should reflect these sequences. In the ideal case the language is a single sequence of patterns that scale from large to small, with the larger scale patterns applying first. Smaller scale patterns are applied to help resolve the unresolved forces in the larger scale patterns.

In a pattern language, or even a sequence, the resulting context of one pattern leads to the context of the next to be applied. No *Solution* completely resolves all of the forces in the pattern. Thus, lower "level" patterns are used to further balance forces. This is why patterns are really only meaningful as part of pattern languages (or at least, pattern sequences).

See Seminars for an example. It is a small pattern language for running short courses.

The original, and still best, example is *A Pattern Language* by Alexander et al.

Format of a Pattern Paper

A pattern paper needs a bit more than just the patterns it discusses. It needs some introductory material giving an overall context and explanation. It may contain reasons why the patterns were developed. It should certainly describe its audience. You may need a references section at the end. As in any paper, credit your sources. It is useful if you say who your audience is. Many papers also include a graphic showing how the patterns in the paper relate to each other.

If your patterns refer to others from the literature, you should include a section at the end that has "thumbnail" versions of those patterns. Sometimes just names and solutions are sufficient for this. Other times, you may need the patlets (problem-solution pairs). If you use implicit meta-data, you will probably need to explain your form somewhere in the paper.

In many papers it is helpful to start each pattern on a fresh page.

Normally other people than the authors helped improve the paper. They should be credited by name. This includes any Shepherd and any Writers' Workshop participants.

See Feedback Patterns for an example.

A paper written for a PLoP conference normally has several patterns, but usually no more than ten. Larger works are submitted in sections to successive conferences.

Understanding Context

Beginning Pattern writers often have a problem getting the Context section right.

Context isn't about your goals or reasons or objectives for the pattern. It is about when you would (as a user) consider applying it.

In pedagogical patterns the contexts are things like

You are a teacher at the very beginning of a course or major topic.

or

You have just returned an exam to your students and several have failed.

or

It is the last day of class.

Continuing with the last one, a Force here might be "You want to be productive on this last day" (a goal). But combining them into a single thing isn't a context.

In Agile Patterns we see something like:

You are forming a new team.

or

You are about to start development of a story.

or

The Customer has just found a flaw.

Notice here, nothing about goals. Just the situation you might find yourself in if it would be worth considering this pattern.

When, just when. Not why or what or how. When.

In a Pattern Language, however, the Context of a pattern includes the results of all of the patterns you have been applied before. This implies some sequencing in their application, of course, which is what makes a Pattern Language a language.

In the published version of Gold Star, the context is given as: You want to encourage excellent work and to praise a student for work well done. How well does that fit the advice here? Can you improve it. Note that several of the Pedagogical Patterns have the same sort of Context. Yes, we sometimes break the rules.

Understanding Problems

The Problem section of a pattern describes something that needs changing in the situation expressed in the Context.

It isn't a question to be answered.

It requires action of some party.

You should be able to express it in a single sentence.

It should be a recurring problem.

The problem should recur in the given Context of the pattern.

It should be a hard problem without an obvious solution.

The problem section may need to contain some explanatory material, but the problem itself should be concisely stated. Find a way to make the concise statement stand out. The use of italic face is helpful. Writing the concise version as the first sentence is also (especially) helpful.

Problem sections typically occur soon after the Context section and before the Forces. Don't give the solution away in your problem statement. The forces immediately follow the problem so that the reader can get a feel for what is going on in solving the problem and can, perhaps, come up with candidate solutions.

If there is an opening story it can occur anytime prior to the forces, but be consistent in your presentation.

Linda Rising, a very experienced author, speaks of the value of hard problems. In reading through the pattern, coming to the end of the problem statement she wants you to ask yourself, "Oh dear, how will I ever solve that." It isn't precisely necessary to write like that, of course, but it makes for good reading. The solution provides release of the tension.

Of course, if you are a subject matter expert for this set of patterns, the problem may have an obvious solution for you. Maybe you are right. Often you are. But it is still a very useful literary technique.

I once took a music course that focused on the classics. The professor suggested that, as we listen to a great piece of music, we try to think about what the next note or phrase should be. Then, when we hear it, to decide whether the composer had a better idea. You can do the same when reading fiction, of course.

Note that there are many published patterns in which the problems are stated as questions. It isn't that this is necessarily a bad practice, but that stating it otherwise is better. Think about why you want that question answered. That may be the key to the problem. Writing it that way strengthens the pattern.

Understanding Forces

The Forces of a pattern are all of those things that the expert must take in to account to come up with the correct solution. Forces are not just the things that push you toward a given solution. They are not just the things you need to overcome. In fact, if the forces all point in the same direction, you probably don't have a pattern. The solution in that case is just "what you do."

Forces push in all directions and with different levels of intensity in a given context. The solution will try to balance these forces as well as possible, but it won't be perfect. The world isn't that simple. Some forces remain at least partly unresolved, even with the best solution.

In writing patterns, it is extremely important that you include all of the forces. This is just simple honesty. If you only include forces that nicely resolve in favor of your favorite solution you are writing propaganda, not patterns.

In the Gold Star pattern we find forces such as

- Students generally want to please the teacher.
- Students want to be rewarded for good work.
- Students don't usually know what the teacher expects.
- Praise can be a motivator.
- Personal tokens of esteem are motivational and sought out.
- Student's don't usually want to be the "teacher's pet."
- Dramatic shifts in a class are remembered.
- Students value consistency and fairness.
- The solution needs to be inexpensive and easy to apply.

Some of these forces suggest that students should get public rewards for doing something the teacher values. Some suggest that the teacher needs to be consistent in rewarding students. Some things suggest you shouldn't overdo it.

Forces are the key to a good pattern. If you don't list the relevant forces, the reader has no way to judge whether the Solution of the pattern is a good one or not. The Forces are the test of the validity of the Solution. In some way the forces are the "why" of the pattern. Why it works.

Understanding Solutions

Just as with the Problem, you should be able to express the Solution in a single sentence. An imperative form is best. Do *This*.

The solution should not be obvious to a non-expert. If it is obvious, you may not have a pattern. Giving Gold Stars to doctoral students (literally, stick-on gold stars) isn't obvious. But it is very effective.

The solution should tell the user what to DO. It is action oriented. It shouldn't tell you to "think about..." or "consider...". If it can't be expressed well in an imperative sentence, it won't be very helpful. The solution shouldn't tell you what NOT to do, but what to DO.

One-quarter inch of drop per linear foot of drain pipe in household plumbing isn't obvious, but it works. It doesn't guarantee that your drains will never clog, but it minimizes clogging. It balances the forces. However, if the drain is supposed to be carrying an especially viscous fluid (crude oil), then the solution will be different, as the forces are not as usual.

If the solution doesn't solve the problem it may be for one of several reasons. You may be trying to do too much in one pattern. The problem is too big, perhaps, or there are several problems hidden in you problem statement. But first-time pattern writers often write a "solution" that is unrelated to the problem stated. A complete mismatch. Sometimes it is just oversight. Sometimes it is because the writer understands the problem all too well and forgets to say everything necessary.

The solution shouldn't, in general, lead to unintended side-effects. If the resulting context is a more complicated situation than the original, your pattern hasn't helped the user. On the other hand, solutions are rarely perfect. They leave some forces partially unresolved.

Most important, the solution should be best practice. One pattern I reviewed recently suggested Closed Book Exams as a solution in a Pedagogical Pattern where the problem had to do with evaluating students in distance learning environments. I think that the context and forces in which this is best practice would be extremely narrow. Yes, this is common practice in education, but that doesn't make it best practice. Closed Book Exams have many unintended side-effects.

Finally, the forces can be skewed in a situation in which you attempt to apply a pattern. I've never tried to use Gold Star in a class in a Boy's Reform School for Violent Repeat Offenders. I'm guessing it could cause problems. The force concerning the reluctance to being a teacher's pet might be especially strong there. The lesson is that you can't apply the solutions blindly, but the lesson for the pattern writer is to work hard to include all of the relevant forces in the pattern.

In some patterns it is useful to have a Caveats section. Here you give the contraindications in which the pattern does not apply or has serious negative consequences. Often the Solution is introduced with **Therefore...**, and the caveats introduces with **However....** This simply points out situations outside the Context of the pattern or situations in which the forces resolve in an unfortunate manner, perhaps because there is an unusual extra force at play. The Fixer Upper Pedagogical Pattern has a few caveats explicitly stated.

Understanding Resulting Context

The resulting context tells us how the solution resolved the forces, but also how it does not. Remaining imbalance in the forces should be resolved in other, smaller scale, patterns that the resulting context should point to.

In a pattern language, the resulting context of one pattern is the context of the next pattern(s) to be applied.

So, the resulting context measures how good the solution is, and if not "good enough" where to look to improve the situation further.

Like the context, the resulting context describes a state of the world. A new state, as the world was changed somewhat in applying the solution.

But no one will believe you if you suggest the solution was perfect in every way, leaving nothing else to do. "Things are good. Really good."

It is harder to write a good resulting context if you are only writing one pattern. The Gold Star pattern was not written with sequences of patterns in mind. There isn't really a resulting context written there. Most teachers will realize the result intuitively, but also that you only partly solve the problem. Students feel a little better. Some students "get it" that you appreciate questions (or whatever). But Gold Star is a very *small scale* pattern that might be made to fit in a lot of small situations.

The Fixer Upper on the other hand explicitly states that the pattern enables students to *actively* work on *larger things* than might be the case otherwise. The resulting context is more important here than in Gold Star since the pattern (as a thing) is larger, and less well known to the average teacher.

Know Your Audience

When writing a set of patterns, make sure you are clear in your mind who the audience is. The audience is those people who might need to apply the patterns to build structure or solve problems. Normally you want to name this audience in the introduction. Sometimes each pattern in a set has a different audience. For example, some patterns in an Organizational Pattern Language might be addressed to managers, others to team leads, others to new hires. You can make this explicit in the Context section of the pattern. If you adopt the "you" form it is especially easy. However, you probably still want to say something about the audience in the introduction.

Then, when you write the pattern, make sure that each part of it is addressed to this audience. It should be written in terms that they will understand and relate to.

One mistake that it is easy to make when writing patterns, or anything, is to implicitly assume knowledge that your reader doesn't have. If you are a subject matter expert, you may think "everyone understands." But they don't. So, it is helpful to tell stories, and to have a good Discussion section somewhere in your pattern. In extreme cases you can have appendices with arcane knowledge that might be needed, or a glossary of important terms.

Another common mistake is to address the different parts of the solution to different people. This is discussed again in the Chapter about the You Form. But the advice can be generalized. Each part should be addressed to the same audience.

Naming Patterns and Telling Stories

One thing that is very useful when experts and budding experts share their experiences is being able to tell stories about good practice in the field. Agile software developers like to sit around and describe what they do to be successful. Effective team builders do the same thing. Questions get asked, advice is given. Expertise is shared.

To enable patterns to be useful in such story telling, it is important that the patterns have names devised with this in mind. Names should be one or two words in most cases: *Gold Star* or *Do Food*. The name can be a noun phrase or a verb phrase, but in a pattern language, the patterns should use the same convention. Not all pattern languages do this, however.

The name can represent the Problem or the Solution. Other things are possible, but these are very common, especially names based on the solution.

In Alexander, the names are mostly noun phrases that describe the thing built (pattern as a thing). When names are verb phrases they can describe how one built the thing.

Names should be clever, but not *too* clever. *Kobayashi Maru* is meaningful to some, but not to everyone. It is probably too clever. It was once the name of a pedagogical pattern that suggests that it is occasionally useful to give students impossible exercises. It's current name is Mission Impossible. Likewise a too clever name for the pattern Keep The Ball Rolling, might be Zorbing.

Take some care that your names aren't culturally biased. The Fixer Upper Pedagogical Pattern has a name that most people in the United States will recognize, but Europeans want some explanation.

Once you have good names, you should also write some stories using them. Some authors include these stories in papers, and many do in books. They are a good way to demonstrate that the patterns are useful in sequence to solve larger problems than those of the individual patterns. But telling these stories, even to yourself, is a useful exercise for the pattern writer, just to test how the names work in conversation.

I included a rather elaborate story in this collection:
http://csis.pace.edu/~bergin/patterns/codingpatterns.html

In *Fearless Change*, the first hundred pages is mostly stories.

Manns and Rising have recommended that you settle on a name relatively late in your process. Keep many *candidate* names and try them out. Once you publish a useful pattern others will adopt your pattern name in their own stories and you will have little freedom to change it thereafter.

This advice is not the same as having a Story section (or sections) within the pattern itself. Story sections are usually shorter and focused on one pattern and how it works in practice. A good practice is to have an introductory story to set up the use of the pattern. The story takes you through to the problem initially. A section like this can appear immediately after the Context. Later in the pattern, after the Solution section, you can finish the story, telling what happened in this mini case-study. It is especially helpful to talk about what was actually done and how the forces were resolved. Manns and Rising make good use of this technique.

Writing in the "You" Form

When you use the YOU form it needs to be consistent.

See Keep The Ball Rolling for an example of a pattern in the you form.

You, the pattern writer, write as if you are speaking to someone (YOU). Make everything consistent with that idea. If the YOU in the pattern refers to different people/groups in different parts, it doesn't work.

Here is an example that doesn't work:

Context: You are a new hire.
Problem: You don't understand the company documentation.
Solution: Write better documentation.

Here the *you* of the solution is someone else, but it reads like "you". Nor is it a problem that can effectively be solved by "you," the new hire. It is a solution for someone else, so the rest of the pattern should be directed at that person.

Generally speaking, the "you" of a pattern is the person who must implement the solution.

But the consistency rule applies even when you aren't using the you form. Make sure every section is consistent with every other. For example, if the problem section describes a problem of one person or group, the solution should address what that group can do to solve the problem or what the person to whom the pattern is addressed can do on behalf of that group or person.

Cultural issues: In some cultures the *you* form is considered impolite. It may be considered "talking down" to an underling. Language in such cultures often compensates for this by having various forms of the word, depending. For example, Spanish, where this is not a cultural issue, has the word usted for speaking to a stranger or brief acquaintance, but tu for speaking to a friend or family member. It is a measure of social distance, but is not hierarchical. Other languages recognize power relationships in the words used for the second person.

Other languages, such as German, use an impersonal form (mann) in some situations. Instead of saying "You should do ...", they might say "One does..."

However, here are two observations. Most patterns, today, are written in English, where there is only one word, and it doesn't have impolite connotations. And, in any case, we do want solutions in patterns to be fairly imperative in nature. The patterns in A Pattern Language (Alexander) are nearly all imperative.

But this is a consideration for those writing for a large audience.

Scope Of A Pattern

Patterns should be as small as possible, but no smaller. (Paraphrasing Einstein)

Don't try to do too much in a single pattern. If you have a large problem, think about smaller problems that need to be solved along the way. Write patterns for the simple ones. Make them work together in a pattern language.

If it is hard to write a solution to your problem that gives concrete advice on what to actually DO in the given context, you may be trying to do too much. If your solution requires a bulleted or numbered list of steps, you are probably doing too much.

If your problem statement is complex, with words like *and* and *or*, split it.

If you have a complex problem to solve, try to tell a story about solving it. Now look for the verb phrases in your story. These may be the core of your patterns.

But, don't forget to generalize when possible. Don't try to be as general as possible at all times, however. Just enough.

Note that in a proper pattern sequence, an early, large scale pattern includes the patterns that follow. And it is included in all the earlier patterns. In *A Pattern Language*, the pattern *House for a Couple* includes all of the Room and Window based patterns. The House pattern can't say everything. The problem is too big.

Small *scope*, however, doesn't necessarily imply small *scale*. In A Pattern Language, the first, and largest scale pattern is Independent Regions, which talks about working toward relatively autonomous cultural regions of 2 to ten million people, covering the earth with around 1000 regions. Its audience is national and regional planners. It is very large scale, but the scope is small. The problem is about cultural cohesiveness. The forces imply that too much bigger or smaller than this won't let culture and economy develop. The next pattern talks about how cities, towns, and villages get distributed within these regions. At the other end of the scale, 250+ patterns later, the scale is less than a square yard (meter). Things From Your Life talks about such things as pictures on your walls being personal, rather than manufactured. The scope is small and now the scale is small as well. But the large scale patterns don't try to solve the small scale problems as well as the large ones.

In organizational or pedagogical patterns, large scale might imply applicability to large groups of people. But large scale might also imply large time scale. In fact, the book Pedagogical Patterns explicitly categorizes the patterns as to time scale: Course as a Whole, ... , Scale of Hours, ..., Scale of Minutes. Several patterns apply at each level of scale, but all have small scope.

Recipes

Recipes aren't patterns. They are too specific.

But, I think it might be possible to develop a pattern language on "feeding a family". It would probably generalize (in one direction) to "feeding any small group of people on a recurring basis". There can be several aspects to such a thing. There are people who need this information (newlyweds, perhaps) and people who have it, though likely few who are sufficiently expert to be able to generalize from their own practice. How would you make it (a) general enough to be used in several cultures and several economic strata, and (b) specific enough to have directions on what to actually "do"? So, perhaps it sounded easy in the first sentence of this paragraph, but turns out to be surprisingly difficult.

But even here, the pattern language would not include any recipes.

Patterns solve recurring problems. When the problems occur they do so in, perhaps, slightly different context, and, usually, with different strength to the various forces. This is why experts are needed to develop the practices that we try to capture as patterns.

Best Practice

Pattern Solutions should give advice on the *best practice* to solve a problem. However, not even experts can know what this is in all cases. But we, as pattern writers, try to discover what that is (though not *invent* it). Patterns are about discovery, not invention.

Sometimes best practice is controversial. Yes, it is best practice, but you don't want to hear that. I was once questioned by a co-author on the pattern Differentiated Feedback, which says that you should give personal feedback to students on their work. Helen Sharp worries a lot about that solution since, as a Professor at Open University (UK), she might teach 2000 people at a time in one course. But, in fact, they do give differentiated feedback, using a large pool of tutors who have some personal contact with the students that the Professor herself cannot.

Here is another example. I'll play with the idea of a pattern language for feeding a family.

Context: It is time to obtain the raw materials for meal preparation.
Problem: I need a mix of fresh and preserved food and it is not immediately to hand.
Solution: Shop every day for that day's main meal.

Compare that with this:

Context: (as above)
Problem: (as above)
Solution: Shop once a week for all the ingredients you will need for that week.

Which of these is best practice? Note that I cleverly omitted the forces. In Italy the first would more likely be thought superior. In the U.S. the second. If you live in the suburbs, it is difficult to shop every day, perhaps. (There might be a higher level pattern at work here, though.) I was once in a situation where it made sense to buy much of the food once a month.

But it should be clear that daily shopping is best and the others are compromised. You eat fresher food, which is healthier. Even better, grow your own.

Can all this be resolved in a single pattern without moving to Italy (yum)? How about a solution along the lines of "Shop on the shortest time scale that makes economic sense." Now, assuming the forces include not just nutrition, but economic issues related to transportation, etc. We see a better resolution.

Many pattern authors, including this one, while striving for best practice can't find it, though we can get what we think is at least good practice. It has become fairly common, following Alexander, to mark our patterns to indicate our confidence in the advice given. A two star pattern indicates that we are certain the advice is best practice. A no star pattern indicates a tentative idea. Once star indicates that we believe that we are on the right track, but not there yet. Gold Star is a two star pattern by the way. So is Differentiated Feedback. Grade It Again, Sam, only has one star, since it is expensive in time to implement. To indicate the star rating, the name can be marked, as in Gold Star **.

Level of Abstraction

Patterns need to be at the "correct" level of abstraction.

Partly this is dependent on the context. Does the same pattern apply in a wider (or different) context? The Gold Star Pedagogical Pattern applies in quite a wide range of contexts. Certainly wider than I envisioned when I wrote it. For example, many managers in business give Gold Stars to their employees. But I didn't re-write it since my overall context was teaching.

In an attempt to write the most general pattern possible, I wrote "Do The Right Thing."

http://csis.pace.edu/~bergin/patterns/dotherightthing.html

Note that I neglected to put in a problem statement. But, beyond that, it isn't really a pattern for the simple reason that it doesn't really tell you what to do. It is too general to give the needed specific advice. In some ways it is the "super pattern" of all others, since each true pattern should resolve in "doing the right thing."

And the problem with recipes is that they are too specific. The author needs to find the right balance in the pattern. When the Manns and Rising book (*Fearless Change*) was being created it was envisioned as a book about introducing "patterns" into organizations. I noticed that nearly all of the patterns that they had written generalized to the introduction of any new idea. So, partly on my advice, they changed the focus, which required re-writing a few of the patterns and adding additional examples. But it made the work much more useful than it would have been otherwise.

A "pattern" can be too specific. Recipes are too specific.

Laws and moral principles are too general to be patterns. The solution is always just "obey the law/principle."

A Pattern In Development

I'm going to try to develop a pattern for creating an artifact, perhaps a pattern, in a group. I'll show you several versions of the "pattern" in development along with discussion of what is "wrong" with the early versions. I won't try for completeness until later, but I hope you get the idea as well as being able to apply the pattern in your own work.

Just Do It

Version 1

Name: Just Do It

Context: You are a member of a team that needs to produce some artifact.

Problem: How do you make good progress?

Forces:

(a) Some people don't help as much as they should.

(b) It is difficult to get agreement on the details of the artifact.

(c) Everyone is terribly busy.

Solution: Plan on doing it yourself and getting whatever help you can from others.

Resulting Context:

(a) The artifact gets built.

(b) Perhaps the team never acted like a team.

(c) You are burned out.

Meta discussion. Is this a pattern? No, for the following reasons. The context is probably fine - it seems pretty general. If I'm not in that situation I can ignore everything else. The problem is stated as a question to be answered, not a problem. It is also probably too general to be covered in a single pattern. *Progress* has many features. The solution is probably too radical to be useful. To see this, examine the resulting (likely) consequence. Have you balanced the forces? Have any of the forces been addressed? Only the drive toward the creation of the artifact has been covered in the solution. There are probably more forces. One that comes to mind is that different people are "available" at different times. Also, the "solution" could tell me more about what to do: "Plan on ..." could be made more direct and helpful - even if it were the "right" solution, which it probably isn't. If the solution is wrong, the name is probably also wrong.

One good thing about this pattern is that it is written in the "you" form, directed to the reader who must apply it. This is a good style for many patterns.

Note that some patterns are named for their solutions (like this one) and some for their problems. There are other ways.

Compare this "pattern" to "common code ownership" in XP (Extreme Programming).

Plan Plan Plan

Here is a new version of the Just Do It pattern:

Version 2

Name: Plan-Plan-Plan -or- Divide and Conquer

Context: You are a member of a team that needs to produce some artifact.

Problem: It will be difficult to create a quality artifact quickly.

Forces:

(a) Some people don't help as much as they should.

(b) It is difficult to get agreement on the details of the artifact.

(c) Everyone is terribly busy.

(d) There is sufficient time if we work effectively - it isn't an impossible task.

(e) Everyone has sufficient skill to contribute something, but not everyone has the same skill.

Solution: Take charge yourself and divide the work among the team members. Take account of people's overall workload, so the work may not be "equal." Notes: You might want to assign yourself a slightly larger or harder portion of the work to avoid resentment.

Resulting Context:

(a) The artifact "mostly" gets built, but it was still difficult to coordinate.

(b) The team "spirit" wasn't really improved. People just did their own task.

(c) Some are burned out, likely yourself, worrying about having it all come together.

Meta discussion: Quality AND Quickly in the problem indicates two problems, not one. Is one of these part of the context? Can you split it in two (or several) patterns? Forces a and b, especially, aren't addressed in the solution. If the artifact can't be divided on "natural" boundaries, this probably won't work. You might be resented for seeming to be the one imposing work. Those who don't normally "give their all" probably won't do so here either. Note that I've focused, in writing these versions, on negative points in Resulting Context. Usually resulting context can be more positive, but "All is well" is never an appropriate resulting context: Problem totally solved, QED.

I've tried to think about more forces here - especially positive or supporting forces. But, in general, forces "push" in all directions. Some toward a given solution and some opposed. Perfect "balance" is normally not achievable. A variation on this solution that has the same spirit is to have an early meeting to divide the work. All YOU need to is make sure this meeting happens and contribute positively to it.

I left the context the same, improved the forces, came up with another "common" solution, but is it the best solution? More to come.

Traveling Artifact

Version 3

Name: Traveling Artifact - or - Keep The Ball Rolling

Context: You are a member of a team that needs to produce some artifact. You have a fixed deadline and the team is dispersed/distributed.

Problem: Due to shaky team dynamics, it will be difficult to create a quality artifact within the required time frame.

Forces:

(a) Some people don't help as much as they should.

(b) It is difficult to get agreement on the details of the artifact.

(c) Everyone is terribly busy.

(d) There is sufficient time if we work effectively - it isn't an impossible task.

(e) Everyone has sufficient skill to contribute something, but not everyone has the same skill.

Solution: Create some version of some part of the artifact yourself and invite your team members to expand and improve it. Do this repeatedly.

Resulting Context: The artifact gets created. Those with the most time, interest, and "drive" do the most work. No one is intentionally left by the way side. It allows for some member(s) to do less, but perhaps that was necessary in any case. A person with a lot of "skill" but little time, can contribute a lot quickly by editing/modifying.

Meta discussion: I changed the context so as to indicate that we were focused on the artifact more than the schedule. I noticed that I've also been assuming, without saying, that the team is dispersed - though it might also work in co-located teams. The name was changed to try to capture this new idea.

It also seems possible to split this into two patterns: "just start" and "continue the process". I focused more on the key issue in the problem, which is that we may not have a smoothly running team with everyone contributing equally. Note that "fairness" was not a force or a goal (problem element) here. I didn't think of the creation of the artifact as a zero-sum game. The forces are the same as version 2.

Sometimes this "meta discussion," which I think of here as comments to the writer, becomes a section of the pattern itself. Part of it anyway. Also. When a problem or solution is more than one sentence long, you should note somehow what is the key idea. Here it is pretty simple, but in general use italics or similar to make it clear. Even better, try to write so that the key idea is the first sentence as I did here.

I think I have better balancing of the forces here and therefore a better solution.

Historical note. A pattern much like this one was used to create and update many of the Pedagogical Patterns. Bergin, Eckstein, Manns, and Sharp passed papers back and forth over many versions. Our problem wasn't the same as here, and the first force didn't apply, but the solution worked out beautifully. We were then in four sites in three different countries. Our problem involved only time and distance. We never actually worked on these in the same location, though we met quite often at conferences and such.

Keep The Ball Rolling

Here is a version using implicit meta-data.

Keep The Ball Rolling

You are a member of a team that needs to produce some artifact. You have a fixed deadline and the team is dispersed/distributed.

Due to shaky team dynamics, it will be difficult to create a quality artifact within the required time frame.

- •Some people don't help as much as they should.
- •It is difficult to get agreement on the details of the artifact.
- •Everyone is terribly busy.
- •There is sufficient time if we work effectively - it isn't an impossible task.
- •Everyone has sufficient skill to contribute something, but not everyone has the same skill.

Therefore: *Create some version of some part of the artifact yourself and invite your team members to expand and improve it.* Do this repeatedly.

- •The artifact gets created.
- •Those with the most time, interest, and "drive" do the most work.
- •No one is intentionally left by the way side. It allows for some member(s) to do less, but perhaps that was necessary in any case.
- •A person with a lot of "skill" but little time, can contribute a lot quickly by editing/modifying.
- •The different writing styles of the team members is also smoothed out somewhat.

-- Image by Josh Berglund (via WikiMedia, License CC-BY)

Tension In Patterns

Here is some advice about writing patterns. Linda Rising is the one who gets credit for this idea.

Maintain some tension in your pattern that is only released (A-Ha) in the Solution.

The Context sets up the story. The problem seems difficult or impossible to solve (don't give away the solution here).

The forces show why this is hard but also point in the direction of the solution (forces in all directions).

The solution reduces the tension (but probably can't remove it completely - hence more patterns at a smaller "scale").

The resulting context points you to "what's next."

The discussion brings it all together.

The known uses show how it has worked out in the past in a variety of situations.

Nothing is revealed about the Solution until you reach that section. Not in the context, or the problem, and only indirectly, implicitly, in the forces.

The patlet should capture it. for example:

(P) Students don't know what is their best behavior for success in your course.
(S) Give 'gold stars' when someone really does the right thing.

The patlet is just shorthand for the pattern and it serves as a quick reminder. It doesn't capture everything, but note that, even here, the problem builds tension and the solution releases it.

Building and releasing tension is a good literary technique. It keeps the reader engaged. The writing isn't "flat". Writing this way moves you from being a journeyman (sorry, sexist), to being a master.

Some authors like to have a section that summarizes the pattern. However, if it comes at the beginning, as it often does, it can easily destroy the tension desired. Putting it late, or last, makes it useful for a second reading of the pattern. Putting all of the pattern summaries at the end of the paper is especially useful. They are in one place and easy to find.

Some would provide a summary, or even a problem statement for the above example like: If you don't give gold stars the students won't know what is their best behavior for success. Here there is nothing left to say. The solution is contained already in the problem. Often just the presence of the word if in a problem statement is an indicator of difficulties with the pattern.

Common Errors

The common errors made by new pattern writers are

Simply forgetting something important. One reason to start with explicit meta-data is to assure that you have at least *something* to say for each major element. If you can't say something about each of the parts, you probably don't have a pattern. Likewise if what you have to say about some element is trivial. Related to this is thinking your unstated assumptions are generally shared.

Too general. When a pattern is too general it doesn't usually give you enough advice about what to do.

Too specific: When a pattern is too specific it is useful only in a small set of situations. A list of things to be done in order is usually an indication of this, though such lists appear in several published patterns. Do this, then do this, then this, etc. It is possibly an indication of one pattern trying to do the work of several, or it is too specific. Try to generalize it. The given list may be an example of how to realize or instantiate a more general solution.

Confusing what goes in the parts: Context, forces, problem can all get mixed up.

Not being clear to someone other than yourself: If you are the expert it is easy to forget that others don't have your specialized knowledge.

Thinking YOUR solution is the only or best solution: Then you are writing propaganda.

Unidirectional forces: In reality, forces point everywhere, not just toward your solution. They also are not just the things that you need to overcome.

Mismatch between problem and solution: This is very common in beginners' work. Read the patlet. Does it make sense apart from everything else?

Not providing a solution that can be realized: The user has to be able to DO something to actually solve the problem. Provide World Peace would be a nice solution, but HOW?

Invention in the guise of patterns: Patterns are not about inventing new solutions, but about capturing the knowledge of the community of experts.

Overly rosy resulting context. "And they all lived happily ever after" only works in fairy tales.

Just like Tai Chi, practice improves you. But ONLY practice improves you. One day's practice gives you one day's progress.

The Process of Writing Patterns

Some expert advice comes from Mary Lynn Manns and Linda Rising

http://csis.pace.edu/~bergin/PatternsWritingPatterns.html

There are at least two ways to write a pattern:

You can work outward from either a Problem that needs solving or a Solution that you recognize as "right" somehow.

(a) Start with the Problem:

In Agile Patterns, the Test First pattern arose from its Problem. The problem was keeping the team writing the correct code in the context of changing requirements and shared code ownership. It was noticed that it was too easy for new code to break old code. This leads you to a solution of regression testing. But correctness of code also implied not writing unnecessary code. This led to test first.

(b) Start with the Solution:

In Pedagogical Patterns, the Gold Star pattern arose from its Solution. I noticed that giving gold stars to students was a really good idea, even if they were older the usual ten years or so. So I started to examine what problem this "solution" was attacking. In essence, I generalized the context in which it was originally used. There was nothing in the forces that seemed to be related fundamentally to age or level.

In the process of mining patterns from existing practice, it is usually the solutions that we notice first. The practitioners may never have actually completely rationalized why they do these things. They probably "know", but implicitly.

In the Keep The Ball Rolling pattern (see pages 18-19), I started with the Problem. The first two versions (Just Do It, Plan Plan Plan) failed primarily due to mismatch between the problem and the solution given.

Get a "patlet" first: a Problem-Solution pair. Make sure they work together. Then think about the rest. Spend a lot of time on the Forces.

Think about the generality of your pattern. Can you make the Context more general?

Think about what applying the solution really does for you. What would you need to also do to use this in a wider context?

Get a lot of feedback. Revise based on what you hear. Don't explain that your readers didn't "get" it. Re-write it so that they do.

Breaking The Rules

I've suggested quite a lot of informal rules for patterns. These sections, in this order; you form; active commands for solutions. Can you break these rules and be successful?

Yes, of course you can. You are the author. The work is yours. The advice is for you, as a beginner, in writing so that you can get started quickly and avoid some obvious pitfalls.

But if you break one of the "rules" here, know why you are doing so. What is it about your material or your audience that requires it. I've shown a few of my own patterns here that break the rules and you can find many more on my web site.

Sometimes, for example, there is a single, overall, context for a set of patterns. There seems to be little reason to repeat it for each one. An introduction early on could explain the context in some detail.

Similarly, a set of patterns written for a dedicated audience who might get nearly everything about a pattern from just the solution and a bit of explanation. Gold Star is like this for educators. They know the forces, though they might not have associated the solution with any problem.

A more radical change is replacing the you form with an I form. Here is the patlet for the Round Robin pedagogical pattern.

You want all students to participate in a discussion.

Therefore, *use a round robin technique to solicit suggestions.*

In the I form it looks like this:

I want all students to participate in a discussion.

Therefore, *I use a round robin technique to solicit suggestions.*

The rest of the pattern would need to be changed to match, of course.

One reason I would consider writing this way is that some cultures treat the you form as impolite. However, most such cultures do have a polite formalism for such situations.

But notice that the you form is very strong with an imperative Solution statement. Most other forms weaken it.

Feedback

The patterns process is designed to give you maximum feedback on your patterns so that you can re-write them effectively.

Typically, published patterns have been re-written at least six times prior to publication. Plan to re-write.

A Shepherd is usually assigned to each pattern paper submitted to a conference. The job of the shepherd is to provide this feedback in an effective way. He or she will try to let you know what they think is good about your work but also what they don't understand, or how they think it can be improved.

Ideally a shepherd is knowledgeable about the subject matter of the paper, but this isn't always possible.

If the shepherd tells you something you don't really want to hear, you can ignore it, but you would do better to consider it as an important piece of information from your audience. If your audience hasn't really "gotten" what you mean, then that is your problem and you have a chance to fix it.

But the shepherd never takes ownership of the paper. It is just feedback. You should consider it, but in your own way.

If you have a shepherd, you are "the sheep", of course. And note that it is the shepherd that chooses the sheep, not the other way around. Potential shepherds "bid" on available papers as part of the conference process. The conference committee makes the match-ups.

After shepherding, a paper is normally "work-shopped." A Writers' Workshop is a group of authors who discuss a paper while the paper's author observes but does not participate. The author hears a discussion of his/her work and can use that to grasp whether the paper was effective or not.

Even if you can't get formal shepherding, you should try to get as much feedback as possible on your patterns (or any writing, actually). You can ask friends and colleagues to review your work and make suggestions. It is especially helpful to know what wasn't understood. But don't just explain it. Re-write the work so it stands on its own.

Shepherding

Here I'll tell you a bit about how a shepherd will approach your paper. This comes from my own experience, having shepherded many papers for PLoP conferences, as well as those of my students. It won't be advice about how to shepherd, however.

I'll assume that the authors are relatively new to pattern writing. Very little of what I'm saying here is likely to apply to an experienced author, though I'll still follow the same process.

The first thing I'll do is read, or at least skim the paper to get an overall feel for what the authors are trying to do. I'll note the form, the general layout, and whether there are aids for the reader, such as an introduction and summary material. I won't be interested too much in the writing style at this point, and certainly not in the form chosen by the authors.

If the paper seems generally sound, I'll proceed to the more technical analysis. But if it seems like the paper is trying to force solutions or has poorly thought out advice, I'll let the authors know immediately of my concerns and suggest a new version. This implies, of course, that I have some knowledge of the subject matter.

Often, I'll need to help the authors break down large "patterns" into something more feasible. For example, if the solution is some kind of list I'll sometimes, depending on the subject matter, suggest breaking it up into parts so that each step is a pattern.

I also might need to ask the authors to focus more on their audience. If there are several patterns, are they directed at the same audience?

If any issues have appeared up to now, a new version may be required before getting in to the details.

Next, I'll note whether the patlets work or not. Does the problem solution pair hold up? Can it stand on its own as an explanation? If not, I'll send the authors back to work to get this much right. I'll recommend hard problems and concise, clear solutions focused on action. Most papers written by new authors have problems here and it may take a while for authors to get it right. I try not to suggest too much, leaving the creativity for them; especially if I'm not an expert in the field. My job is not to make spelling and grammar corrections. Authors writing in languages other than their native one, should seek help from a native speaker to get this right, but it isn't really the shepherd's job.

Once the patlets work, I'll probably next look at whether the various ideas in the patterns are correctly categorized. Is this really a force, or a context, etc. I'll also look at the generality of the context, and the completeness of the forces. If the forces seem unidirectional, it will require changes. Even more important is the completeness of the forces. Are there missing forces?

Normally, I'll give general advice on some things. Linda Rising's advice about settling late on the names is usually passed on, for example. Does the paper need (more) examples or more stories?

Once the authors have reached the stage at which none of the above turns up issues, the work is starting to look like real patterns, and the advice depends on the paper itself. The authors can focus on smaller things like getting the language right and making sure the explanations are clear. They can finalize the names and the form, perhaps.

The shepherd will try to get his or her comments back to you within a few days of receiving a version. Shepherding for the PLoP conferences is normally about three or four cycles of versions and comments over a month's time. You should try to get a new version to the shepherd within a few days of receiving comments.

Everything said so far assumes the shepherd has some domain knowledge. Committees try to match shepherds taking this in to account. It isn't always possible, however, and occasionally a shepherd will get a paper about which they know little. Here it is a little harder to comment on anything besides the form and language. However, the shepherd needs to be assured somehow that the authors have the required expertise and that they aren't trying to impose a pattern form on invention or propaganda.

Workshops

If you submit your paper to a PLoP (Pattern Languages of Programming) conference, it will first be assigned to a Shepherd for improvement. After a few weeks it may be accepted for a Writers' Workshop at the conference.

The workshop process was introduced to the patterns community by Richard Gabriel, who is a poet as well as a computer scientist. The process is used extensively by poets to improve their work.

A workshop consists of half a dozen or so authors, who have very recently read the paper to be workshopped. They will come to the workshop with a marked-up copy, detailing their potential comments to the author. The author (or at least one, if there are several) of the targeted paper is present but does not participate in the main discussion unless addressed directly. The participants discuss the paper using some standard process such as the following.

Someone says a few words about what the paper is about. Others may amend or extend the remarks.

Participants then talk about what is good in the work, stressing what they believe should be retained in a future version.

The longest section is a discussion of problems and suggested improvements. The participants talk to each other, not to the author. They try to target what isn't understood or is confusing. They may mention technical issues in the paper.

Meanwhile, the author is listening and taking notes, but is not allowed to defend the paper or the ideas. The author is a "fly on the wall."

There is a moderator so that the participants don't get into arguments about things. The author just notes that there was disagreement and the workshop moves on. Nor does the moderator like to permit participants just restating what someone else said.

At the end, the author is allowed to ask for clarification of comments made, but, again, not to defend the work.

The members of the workshop then thank the author and give him or her their marked up versions. It is helpful if their names are on the paper, so that the author can contact them for more clarification. The author should note the names of the members in any case, for inclusion in the acknowledgements.

Finally the author produces a new version taking into consideration what was said.

The value of a workshop is the feedback provided by the audience of the paper. If the audience "hears" something different than what the author intended, the author has a chance to improve the presentation so as to be more clearly understood.

Sample Patterns

Here are a few sample patterns from different languages. They are included to illustrate different forms.

Singleton Password

Synopsis: For high-risk accounts, use individual passwords.

-

Some accounts are so precious that misuse must be avoided in any case. Passwords aren't really the best way to do this, but if you are lacking any other mechanism, you have to come up with an as-secure-as-possible password.

Therefore, *choose a complicated password that is used for exactly this one account and no other.* A complicated password, at the time of writing this pattern, is probably an arbitrary combination of letters and digits of a minimum length like 8 characters.

This was written in about 2002. The idea is still sound, but not the suggestion of 8 character passwords. The overall pattern language was about creation and maintenance of a set of secure passwords. The audience is those with a bit of technical sophistication. Therefore the form is very minimal. There were 16 patterns in 10 pages. It was included in EuroPLoP 2002. It was an online collaboration of six authors.

The following pattern comes from my elementary Java programming patterns. The overall context is that you are a novice learning to write Java code and the overall problem is that it is not obvious how to write good code.

(6) Logical Interface (Maintainability) **

A program is most adaptable if it is can easily be thought of and read in the terms of the problem it solves, rather than the solution it provides. When you write a class you do so to solve some problem, and you use some internal implementation to represent the solution. If the only way to understand the class is to think of it as manipulating the implementation you will too often need to get mired in detail of the state changes. If, however, you can consider it in terms of the services it provides to clients and in the terms of the original problem, it is more likely that you can take an overview that obscures the detail so that you can get the "big picture".

The interface of a class (its public methods) gives the best overview of the class and what it does. This is the set of services it provides to its clients.

Therefore, *the interface of your class should define its logical services, not its implementation*. If your public methods consist (largely) of accessors and mutators for individual fields, you have probably not adhered to this rule.

In particular, if you have "designed" a class by first deciding what fields it needs and then providing accessors/mutators for these, you do not have the basis for a maintainable program. The client must then think in terms of your implementation, not in terms of the logic of the application. Worse, if the implementation changes, you will be tempted to change the mutators/accessors also, since you have developed this mind set about design. Then the client code will also need to change. This will perhaps result in further changes that will propagate throughout the code. This is a maintenance nightmare.

In Java, the interface of a class can actually be a Java interface. If you design this way, you will be less likely to fall into the implementation first trap.

Sometimes the best way to proceed is to examine how a typical client will need to interact with the class you are developing. You might even write some test code that the client might incorporate. This can give you a guide to a logical interface. The client won't want to know about the internals of your class and will want to express things in its own terms. However, don't try to anticipate all client uses or you may build something that is too specialized. In extreme programming such test code, written before the class is developed, is a fundamental part of the methodology. See http://extremeprogramming.org for example.

In the above, the (6) is just the pattern number and the two *'s indicate that I think this is an essential pattern: you can't write good code without doing this. The patterns were categorized: Design, Maintainability, Style, etc.

The style here is more tutorial than formal. The problems, beyond the overall problem, are inferred. Everything up to the Solution (introduced with the word **Therefore**) is context, problem, and forces, presented as a discussion. Everything after is about implementation of the solution.

The next pattern is from the book Pedagogical Patterns. The sections are separated by *** and the problem and solution are in bold. Examples and implementation appear in italic face. The context states a goal and is, therefore, not the best statement possible. I think a better context statement would be: "You are teaching a course and a student has just done something you'd like other students to also do."

Gold Star **

Feedback Patterns

This pattern is based on Gold Star, written by Joe Bergin and revised by Helen Sharp.

You want to encourage excellent work and to praise a student for work well done.

***

Students want and need your praise. Praise can be a prime motivator, and students work best when they feel good about themselves and feel appreciated. If other students see what you value, they may be motivated to focus on these things too.

Normally the reward structure is private. In grading you give the student praise, but this loses the opportunity to show other students what you value most highly.

***

Therefore, when a student is doing well, or has done something well, praise them *publicly* **for it.**

Achievements you might consider rewarding include an especially good job on a project or a special contribution to a class, or to campus life in general. Give a public token of appreciation for work well done. As known by every elementary school teacher, this works for young children. It is often unexpected by young adults, and this alone can account for some of its effectiveness.

The token can be a few simple words spoken in public to the class or it can be an insertion into the student's permanent academic record.

If you are going to do this, it is important to be consistent, and never belittle a student for poor work.

You also need to be sensitive to the students and their likely reactions. This approach will work better in some cultural settings than in others.

You might consider publishing the student's work on the course website, in which case this pattern is complementary to **Student Online Portfolios**.

***

There are a variety of ways of implementing this pattern. If a course is difficult, then you could try publishing "Gold, Silver and Bronze Medal" winners on the Internet. If your college policy allows you to insert a special note into a student's permanent file when they do something out of the ordinary, then this is worth pursuing. Students value such notes highly.

At a lower level, you could keep to hand a handful of sticky gold stars (like those used for young children). These could be handed out to students in the class for special work, such as asking key questions. You could choose to make your reward very public or private.

Joe Bergin gives these sticky stars to students at all levels, including Doctoral students. He has noticed that he gives most stars for asking questions.

Here is a pattern from *Agile Software: Patterns of Practice*. Referenced patterns in the collection are shown in bold. Note the section separators. First part is context. After the ??? is the problem statement. The arrow glyph introduces forces, and !!! the solution. The overall audience of the book is teams/developers/organizations getting started with Agile Software Development.

Just Start

You are organizing a new project, perhaps taking a manager role or technical lead. You are spending a lot of time trying to get started on the first project.

???

Sometimes the organization can take forever in trying to make decisions on how to start a new project with a new methodology. Everyone needs to understand how it will work. Everyone seems to want to wait until all questions are answered.

⟷

• Many teams starting agile are still stuck in the mode of trying to gather all requirements before you begin.

• There may be fear of failure among many participants.

• Working software is the best proof of any new methodology.

• Agile processes can be tuned as you go, both the direction of the project itself, and the practices of the team and the stakeholders. Nothing needs to be decided only once in an agile project.

• It is hard to make big and expensive errors in an agile project, other than ignoring what you know must be true.

!!!

Therefore, *just start the project and let everyone learn through the first couple of iterations how it works and what its tradeoffs are.* If you learn it was a mistake, you won't have spent a lot of time and money.

• This can be risky, and someone needs to put up some initial funding to make this happen. A **Nano-Project** might be a safer way to begin.

• Make sure you have an **Effective Coach** or **ScrumMaster** to guide these initial iterations so that the practices are learned and the stakeholders can get more comfortable with the process.

The author worked on a project that spent months in discussion, followed by a nearly equal project phase. The team could have been finished in half the time, or delivered twice what they did. Nothing important was actually decided or changed in this initial discussion period. Finally they realized that if they didn't Just Start they would never end.

The following Pedagogical Pattern uses explicit meta-data. It was written for a very specific purpose. It would generalize nicely. This older (for the Pedagogical Patterns Project) format, doesn't give a Solution. Instead note the Structure section. In my view the advice here is sound, but it could do with a re-write into a more modern form that would make the ideas clearer.

Name

Brainstorming

Short description/Intent

To introduce organizational techniques CRC analysts use to discover classes.

Applicability

The Brainstorming pattern introduces a key technique used in CRC Card Analysis.

Consequences

The brainstorming pattern:

* provides a method for early discovery of candidate classes in a new system
* encourages students to recognize the importance of group interaction in early analysis stages
* lets instructors make the class discovery process tangible
* may be resisted by technology oriented students who view people skills as peripheral or time consuming

Example Instances

Used to teach class discovery in applications including: stock market, ATM machines, traffic light control.

Implementation

* exercises can be difficult to implement if the available population is not diverse
* many references are to literature outside of computer science (but see "The CRC Card Book" by Bellin & Simone (Addison-Wesley)
* instructors with industry experience are likely to have more success with this pattern
* flipcharts and markers are essential aids to the process
* don't criticize ideas; don't laugh at other participants suggestions
* one person must serve as the scribe (whoever writes the fastest!)
* pattern excludes revision of candidate classes (see related Role Playing pattern)

Motivation

Students in CS programs often have a difficult time applying group interaction techniques. This is because typical instruction, even that which uses group projects, does not simulate many industry meeting situations. Brainstorming techniques based upon social psychological research have been proven effective when applied in a specific fashion by OO analysts in discovering classes in a new system.

Structure

Step 1: Review Brainstorming Principles:
All Ideas Are Potential Good Ideas, Think Fast and Furious First, Ponder Later, Give Every Voice a Turn, A Little Humor Can Be a Powerful Force
Step 2: State Session Objectives
Step 3: Use a Round Robin Technique
Step 4: Discuss and Select Candidate Classes

Author

David Bellin

Here is an old form of Gold Star, using a format such as the above. When it was redone in the modern form it was rethought as well. The forces were improved, leading to a preference for public, rather than private displays in the solution.

Name

Gold Star

Short description/Intent

Students should get praise for what they do well.

Contraindications

If you are going to do this, then don't forget to be consistent.

Example Instances

My compiler course is seen as very difficult. As an added incentive, I publish the "Gold, Silver, and Bronze Medal" winners each year on the internet.

http://csis.pace.edu/~bergin/compiler/CompilerAward.html

When bumping into a student in the halls or elevator, you can mention how much you liked the solution they provided in the previous assignment (if indeed you did). Simple things like this can (and do) change lives.

Dartmouth College had (has?) a policy that a professor can insert a special note into any student's permanent file when they do something out of the ordinary. This might be an especially good job on a project or a special contribution to a class or to campus life in general. These notes are highly valued by students.

An extravagant example of this is when a professor publishes a student's best work on a course web page.

The name, of course, comes from a fairly common practice in elementary school in which a teacher will put a gold star on well done papers. Some teachers have special ink stamps made with special sayings for their students. I actually pass out a few gold stars in each course (available in any good stationery store), mostly for asking really key questions. I make this very public.

You can give chocolate or other candy treats for the best presentation.

Implementation

This works for young children as every elementary school teacher knows. It is often unexpected by young adults, and this alone can account for some of its effectiveness.

Indications

Students look up to professors as role models. They want and need our praise. Praise can be a prime motivator. Especially when it comes from someone who is respected.

Students work best when they feel good about themselves.

Students, like their professors, like to feel appreciated.

Problem

Sometimes students amaze us in class or in their turned-in work. Normally the reward structure is very private, which is fine, but then we lose the opportunity to show other students what we value most highly.

References

None given

Resources Needed

Something to use for a token.

Solution

When students do something well, praise them for it.

Give a token of appreciation for work well done. This can occur either publicly or privately. It can be a simple few words spoken in private or it can be an insertion into the student's permanent academic record.

The forces at play here also suggest that you should never belittle a student even for poor work.

User category

All students at all levels.

Author

Joseph Bergin

Here is an abstracted version of the Singleton pattern from Design Patterns: Elements of Reusable Object-Oriented Software. This may have been the first use of explicit meta-data. There is no problem statement. Problems are inferred from the Intent and Motivation sections. In the book, each pattern is about ten pages long.

Name:

Singleton

Classification:

Object Creational

Intent:

Ensure a class only has one instance

Motivation:

It is important that some classes only have a single instance.

Applicability:

Use the Singleton Pattern when ...

Structure:

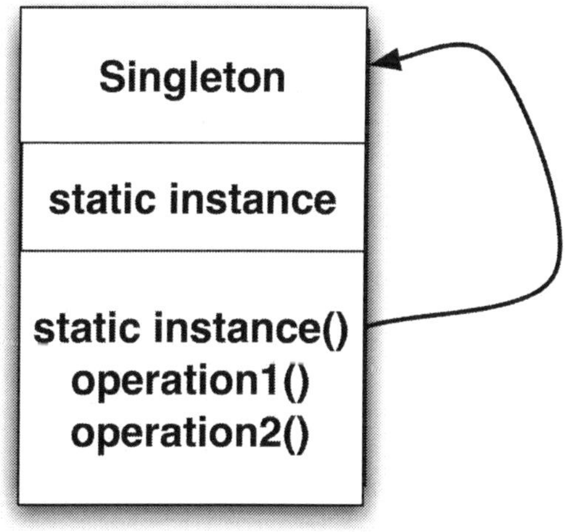

(updated and adapted from original)

Participants:

Singleton

- defines an instance operation to retrieve the unique instance...
- more

Collaborations:

Clients access the instance solely through Singleton's instance operation.

Consequences:

1. *Controlled access to a single instance...*
2. *Reduced name space...*
3. *more - omitted*

Implementation: Omitted

Discussion omitted. Original shows "code" in Smalltalk and C++ using abstract names.

Sample Code:

omitted - original shows and discusses a MazeFactory class in C++. Code is more concrete than in the Implementation section.

Known Uses:

Several given, omitted

Related Patterns:

Many other patterns are implemented using Singleton, including: Abstract Factory, Builder, Prototype.

Thumbnails

Here are a few thumbnails of pedagogical patterns so that you can get an idea. These are written in a form to emphasize the solution of the pattern, but there are other possibilities. The original paper on Feedback Patterns needed to reference these (and others), so we included the thumbnails.

Build and Maintain Confidence

How do you challenge students to develop their own solutions? Students expect the one and only right solution to a problem from the instructor. But often there is no single answer, but many equally correct answers.

Therefore, present a problem taken, as in Solution Before Abstraction from the domain of the students. Provide some hints via questions that have to be answered and that may lead to a solution.

Explore for Yourself

A person's success is based mainly on her ability to learn new concepts efficiently and to act as a team player by sharing knowledge and insights. You want to give your students the ability to learn in the future and to communicate their wisdom, but students are often afraid of taking responsibility for their own learning.

Therefore, assign topics to the students that they have to learn on their own and ask them to present the topic afterwards. It is helpful to provide hints for resources related to the topic.

Different Approaches

Communication always takes place between a sender and a receiver, and the effectiveness of communication isn't measured by what the sender says, but by what the receiver understands. Every person obtains information differently, using different sensory modalities. Some people, the visuals, learn most effective by watching; the auditory learners, by listening; and the kinesthetic learners, through action. Be aware: Not every student uses the same sensory modality as you!

Therefore, provide different approaches to the same topic. Accept different learning styles by addressing various sensory modalities. It might be difficult to provide different approaches for every single topic, but make sure to at least change the approach when you change the topic.

Sources

Pedagogical Patterns discussed here can be found in:

Bergin, Eckstein, Manns, Sharp, Marquardt, Chandler, Sipos, Völter, Wallingford (eds), *Pedagogical Patterns: Advice For Educators*, Joseph Bergin Software Tools, 2012, ISBN 9-781479-171828. Available in print at amazon.com and in epub and kindle formats.

Much of the source material for the book can be found at http://csis.pace.edu/~bergin, including the Feedback Patterns.

Agile Software Development Patterns can be found in:

Joseph Bergin, *Agile Software: Patterns of Practice*, Joseph Bergin Software Tools, 2012. Available at http://cafepress.com/jbergin.

Both the above books are available in print and in electronic formats (ePub and Kindle) at the iTunes music store and at Amazon.

The Fearless Change book is an excellent source for organizational patterns:

Manns, Rising, *Fearless Change: Patterns for Introducing New Ideas*, Addison-Wesley, 2005, ISBN 0-201-74157-1

Richard Gabriel has written a book about workshops:

Richard P. Gabriel. *Writers' Workshops & the Work of Making Things: Patterns, Poetry...*, Pearson Education, 2002, ISBN 978-0201721836

The original pattern language is

Alexander, Ishikawa, and Silverstein, *A Pattern Language: Towns, Buildings, Construction,* Oxford, 1977, ISBN 0-19-501919-9

The first generally recognized book of software patterns is

Gamma, Helm, Johnson, Vlissides, *Design Patterns: Elements of Reusable Object-Oriented Software*, Addison-Wesley, 1995, ISBN 0-201-63361-2

Ward Cunningham has been instrumental in bringing patterns to the software community. He has written on his suggested method of writing Pattern Languages: http://www.c2.com/cgi/wiki?TipsForWritingPatternLanguages

The Seminars Pattern Language can be found at: http://seminars.fed.wiki.org/view/welcome-visitors/view/contents

Made in the USA
Monee, IL
04 November 2026

67378109R00026